WRECK AND DESTROY THIS JOURNAL

MATERIALS

- CREATIVITY
- IDEAS
- SPONTANEITY
- PEN
- PENCIL
- GUM
- STICKERS
- GLUE
- WATER
- SALIVA
- SMELLS
- TEA/COFFEE
- WHITE THINGS
- BALL
- NEWSPAPER
- EMOTIONS
- DIRT
- NEEDLE
- SCISSOR
- HANDS
- FOOD
- SHOES
- STAPLES
- TIME
- TAPE
- TEARS
- INK
- SPOONS
- PHOTOS
- FOUND ITEMS
- PAINT
- INK

Are You Ready?

THIS BOOK BELONGS TO:

WRITE YOUR NAME ILLEGIBLY

WRITE YOUR NAME LOWERCASE

WRITE YOUR NAME UPPERCASE

WRITE YOUR NAME BACKWARD

WRITE YOUR NAME VERY FAIWTLY

ADDRESS:

PHONE NUMBER:

EYE COLOR

During the wrecking this book

you will get dirty. you may find yourself

with in dirt and paint.

you gonna be get wet. you might get

aggressive.

Be careful when try to wreck this journal

and don't hurt yourself!

INSTRUCTIONS

1. TAKE THIS JOURNAL WHEREVER YOU GO
2. FOLLOW THE INSTRUCTIONS ON EVERY PAGE
3. INSTRUCTIONS ARE OPEN TO INTERPRETATION
4. PUSH YOUR BRAIN TO FIND DIFFERENT WAYS TO WRECK!

Have Fun!!

Use this page as a TEST PAGE

For every color you can get your hands ON.

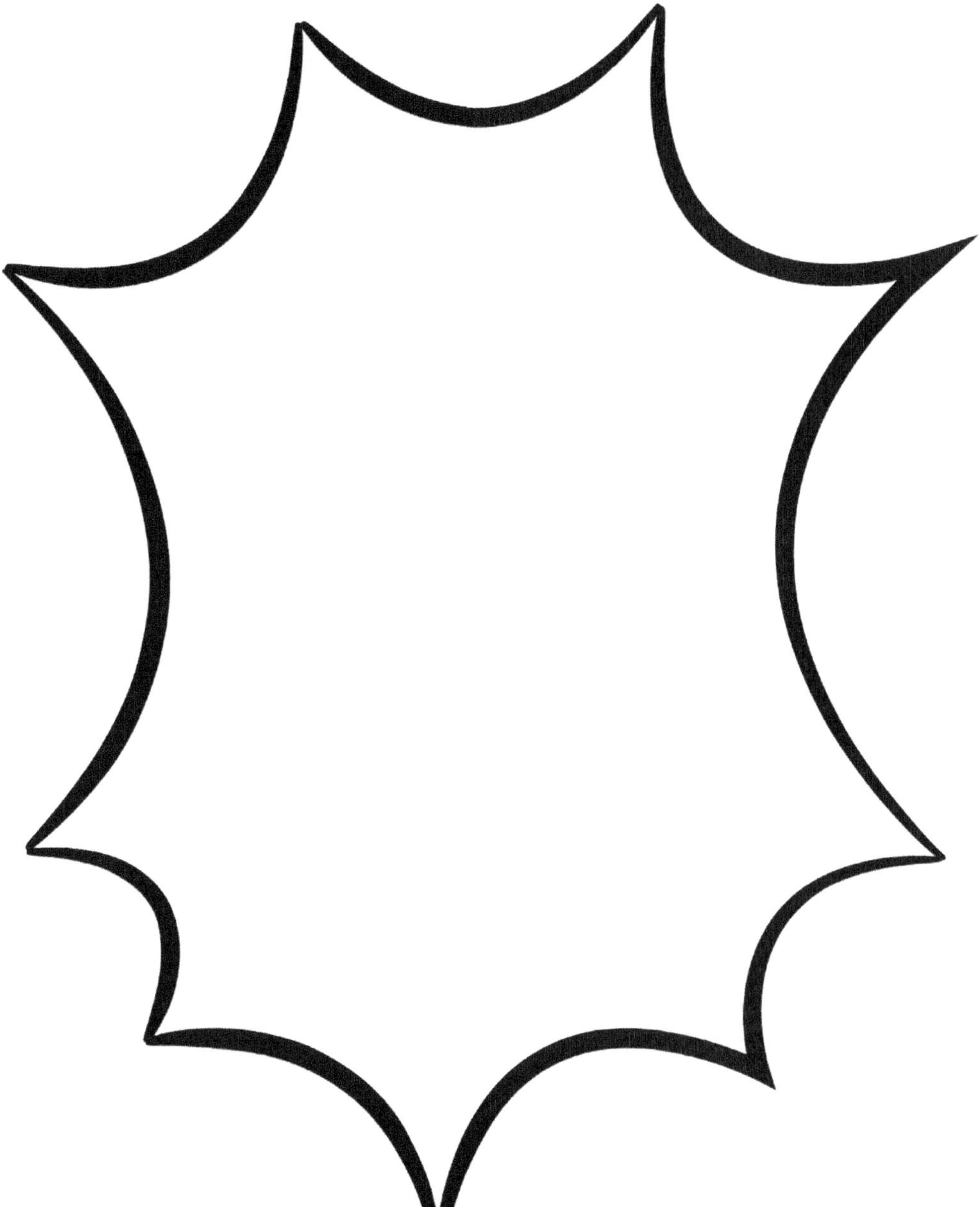

ADD YOUR OWN PAGE NUMBERS ANYWHERE YOU WANT

STARTING HERE

CRACK THE SPINE

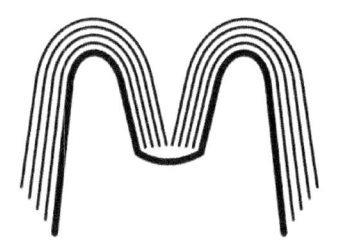

COLOR THIS PAGE
RED
ON PURPOSE.

POUR, SPILL, DRIP, FLING YOUR COFFEE HERE.

POKE HOLES IN THIS PAGE USING A PENCIL

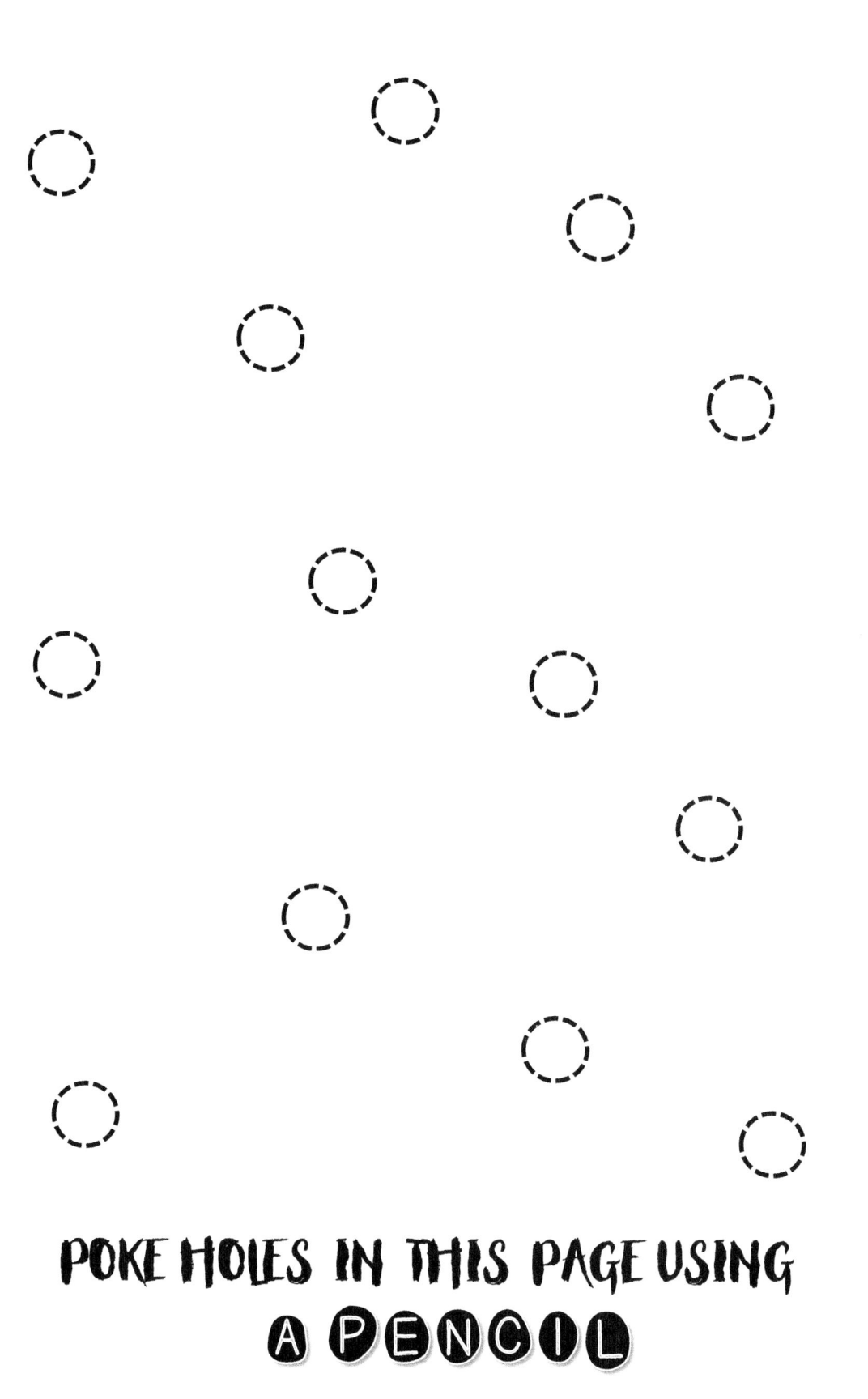

DRAW FAT LINES AND THIN.
Pushing Really Hard With The Pencil.

THIS PAGE IS FOR
HANDPRINTS OR FINGERPRINTS
GET THEM DIRTY, THEN PRESS DOWN

Color This Entire Page.

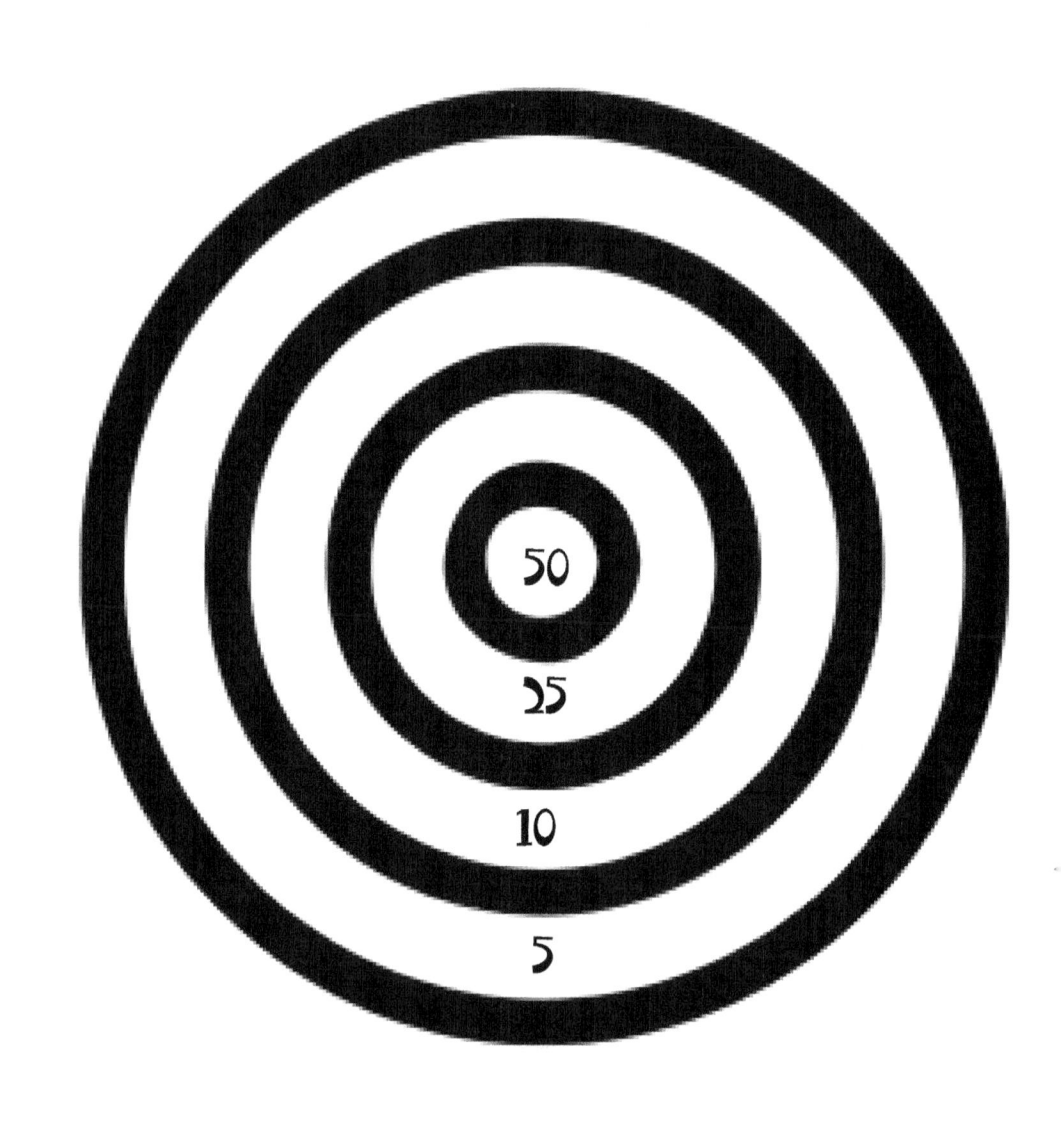

THROW SOMETHING
A PENCIL, A BALL DIPPED IN THE PAINT.

PRESS LEAVES AND OTHER FOUND THINGS.

do some rubbings with a pencil crayon.

FIGURE OUT A WAY TO

FREEZE.

this page.

Roll The Journal Down A Large Hill.

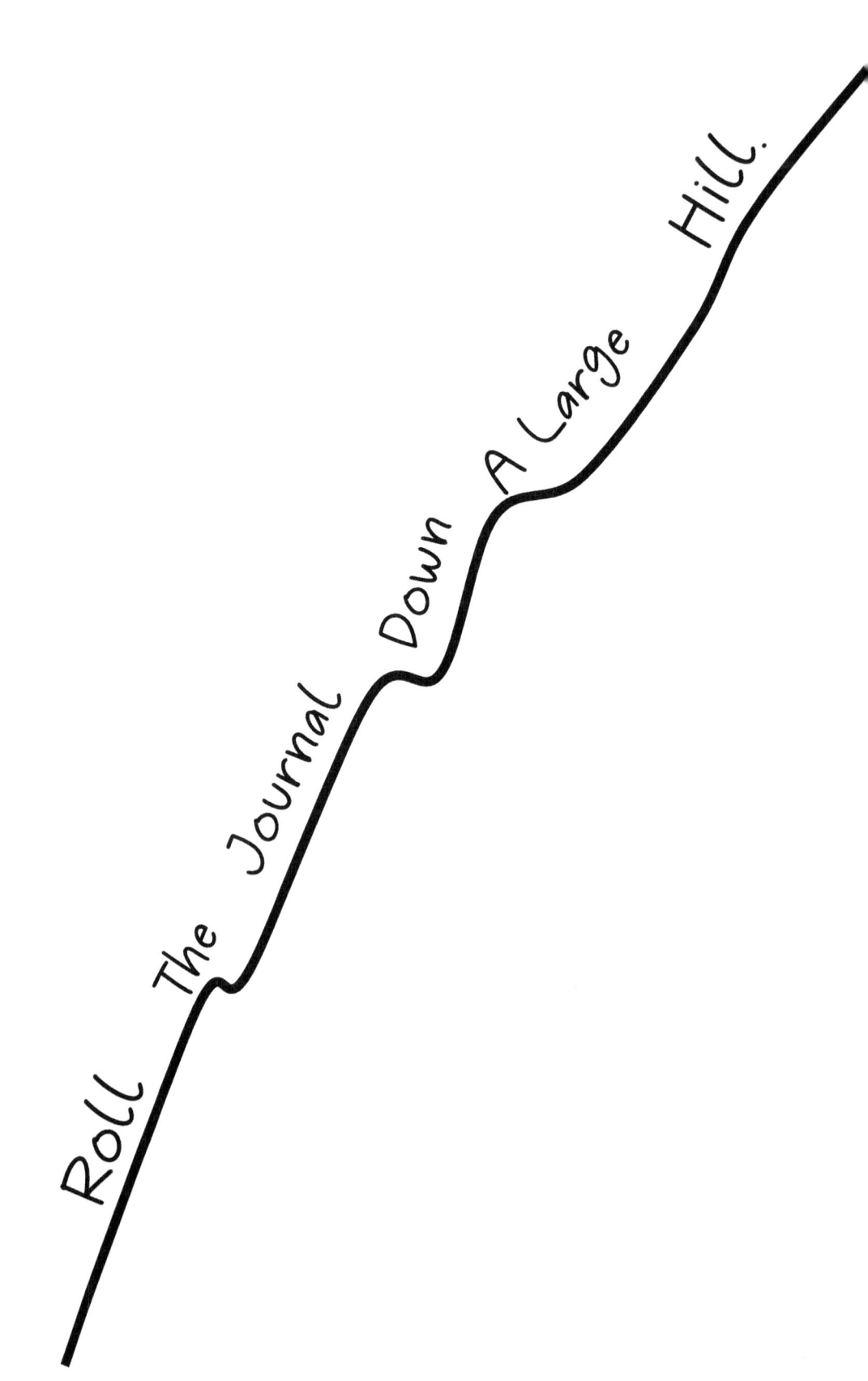

FLOAT THIS PAGE

COVER THIS PAGE

WITH WHITE THINGS.

Doodle Over Top Of

- ◯ THE COVER
- ◯ THE TITLE PAGE
- ◯ THE INSTRUCTIONS

FOLD DOWN THE CORNERS OF YOUR FAVORITE PAGES

fill in this page when you are really ANGRY

Turn this page black

WRITE A LIST OF MORE WAYS TO DESTROY THIS JOURNAL.

1.

2.

3.

4.

5.

6.

7.

8.

9.

10.

11.

12.

Draw lines
Writing utensils
(Sticks, spoons, twist ties

ABNORMAL
Dipped in ink or paint.
Comb,etc.)

COVER THIS PAGE IN TAPE (CREATE SOME KIND OF PATTERN).

Glue, Staple, or Tape These PAGES Together.

WRITE OR DRAW WITH

YOUR LEFT HAND.

Hang the journal in public place. INViTE PEOPLE tO DRAW HERE.

WRITE ONE WORD

OVER AND OVER.

Place Sticky Things Here. (honey, gum, syrup, glue, sucker, marshmallow)

TEAR STRIPS RIP IT UP!

RUB Here WITH DIRT

DRIP SOMETHING HERE.
(Ink, Paint, Tea)
Close The Book To
Make A PRINT.

DRAW LINES WITH YOUR PEN OR PENCIL.
Lick Your Finger And Smear This Lines

COLLECT THE STAMPS OFF
Of All Your Mail.

COLLECT FRUIT STICKERS HERE.

STICKERS YOU FIND ON BOUGHT FRUIT.

FILL THIS PAGE

WITH CIRCLES

JOURNAL GOLF

1. Tear out page, crumple into a ball

2. Place journal into a triangle shape

3. Hit/kick the ball through the triangle

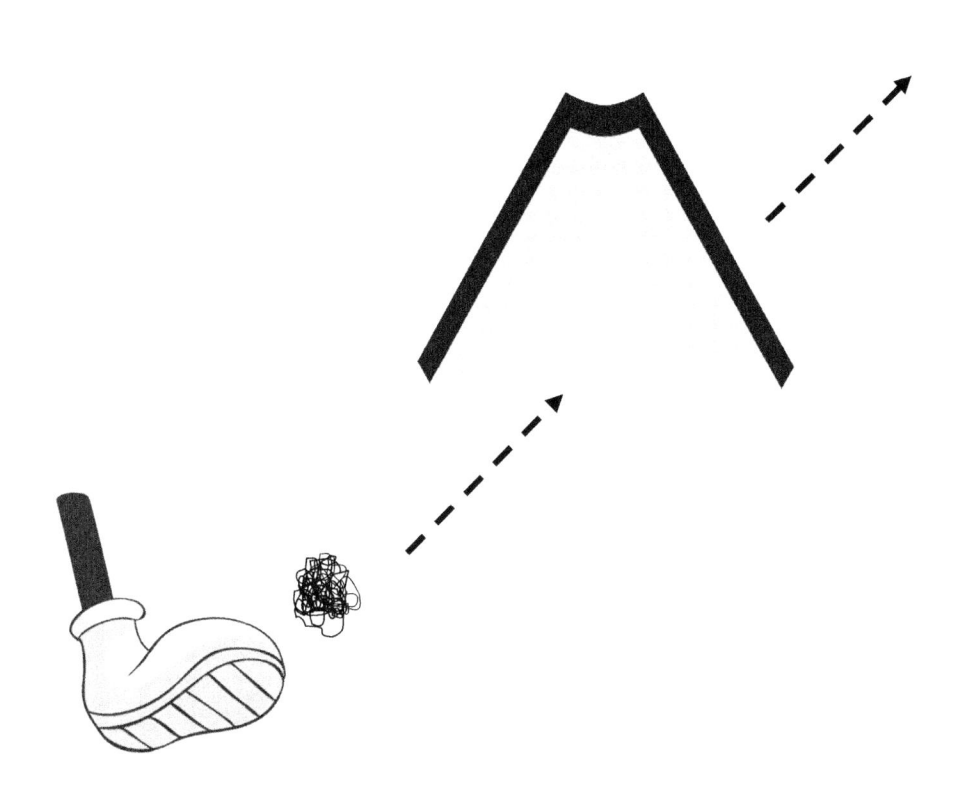

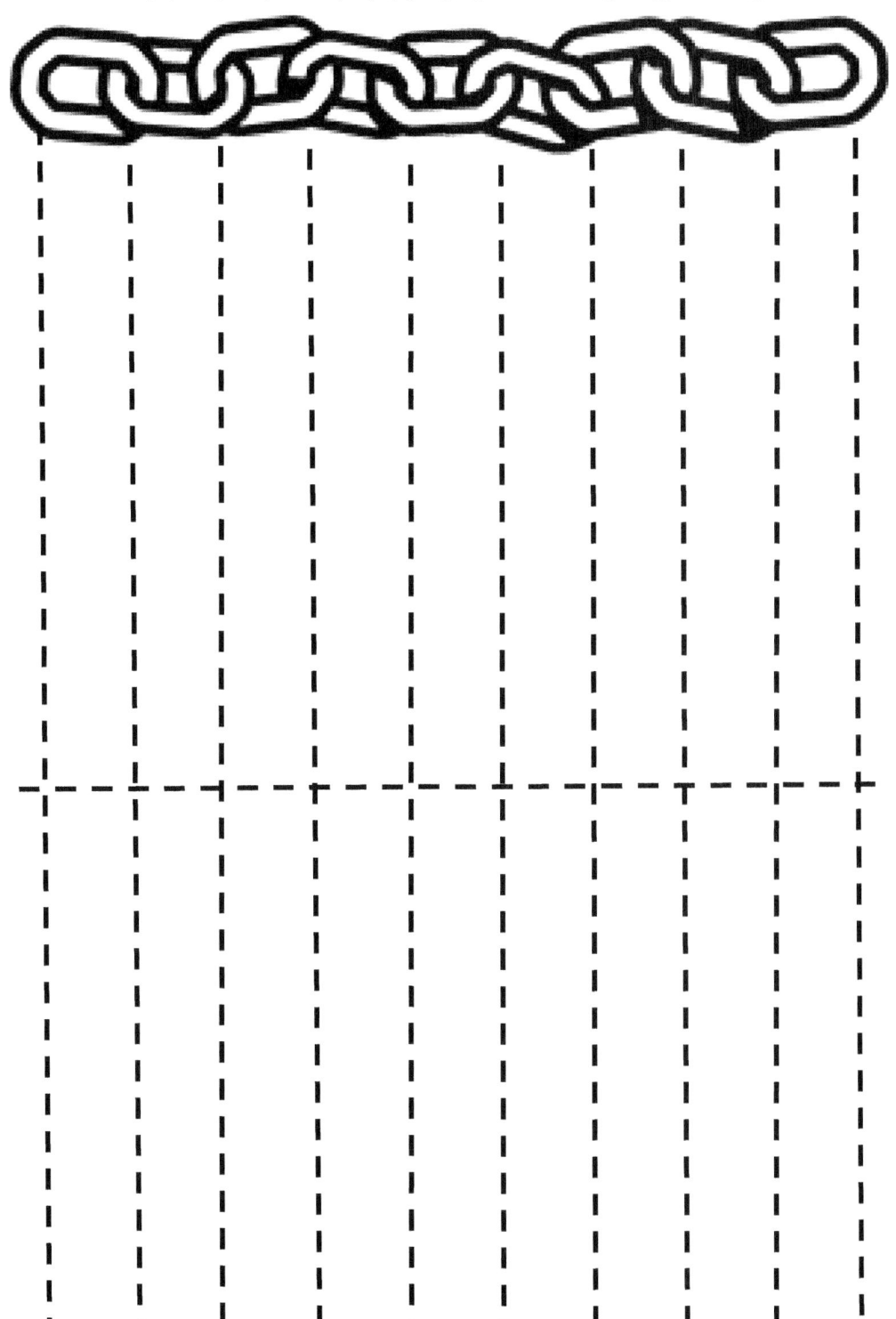

MAKE A PAPER CHAIN.

This page is a sign.
What do you want it to **say?**

TRACE YOUR HAND.

Close
The Journal.

WRITE/SCRIBBLE SOMETHING

ON THE EDGES.

BRING THIS BOOK IN THE SHOWER WITH YOU

STAND HERE
Wipe your feet, jump up and down

TONGUE PAINTING 👅

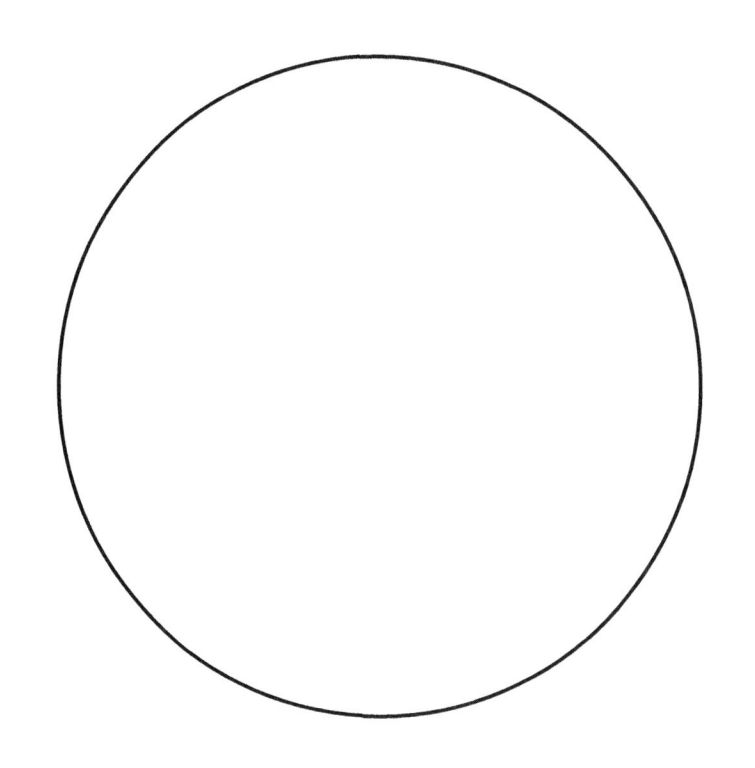

1. Eat Some Colorful Candy.
2. Lick This Page.

TEAR OUT CRUMPLE.

Infuse this page with a **SMELL** of your choosing.

Write with the pen in your mouth.

Glue a random page from a newspaper here.

FIND A WAY TO WEAR THE JOURNAL.

Give away your Favorite PAGE.

Smush Something Colorful Onto THIS PAGE.

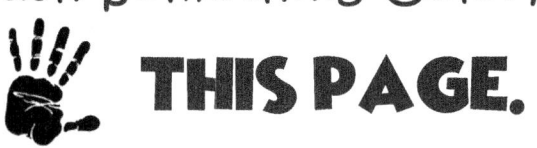

HIDE A secret message somewhere in this book.

Sew This Page

Chew on this.

WARNING: DO NOT SWALLOW

Turn The Book Into a Shoe.

sdrawkcaB etirW

GLUE RANDOM ITEMS HERE.
(i.e., things you find in your couch, on the street, etc)

DRUM ON THIS PAGE WITH PENCILS.

A place for your Grocery lists.

DO A REALLY
(Use Ugly Subject,

UGLY DRAWING
(Gum, Dead Things)

WRITE SOME THOUGHTS.
 COVER UP THESE THOUGHTS
 WITH THE COLOR OF YOUR CHOICE.

MAKE A SUDDEN, DESTRUCTIVE, UNPREDICTABLE MOVEMENT WITH THE JOURNAL

Start

Create a non-stop Line.

MAKEUP	DRINKS	NATURE	VARIOUS

STAIN LOG

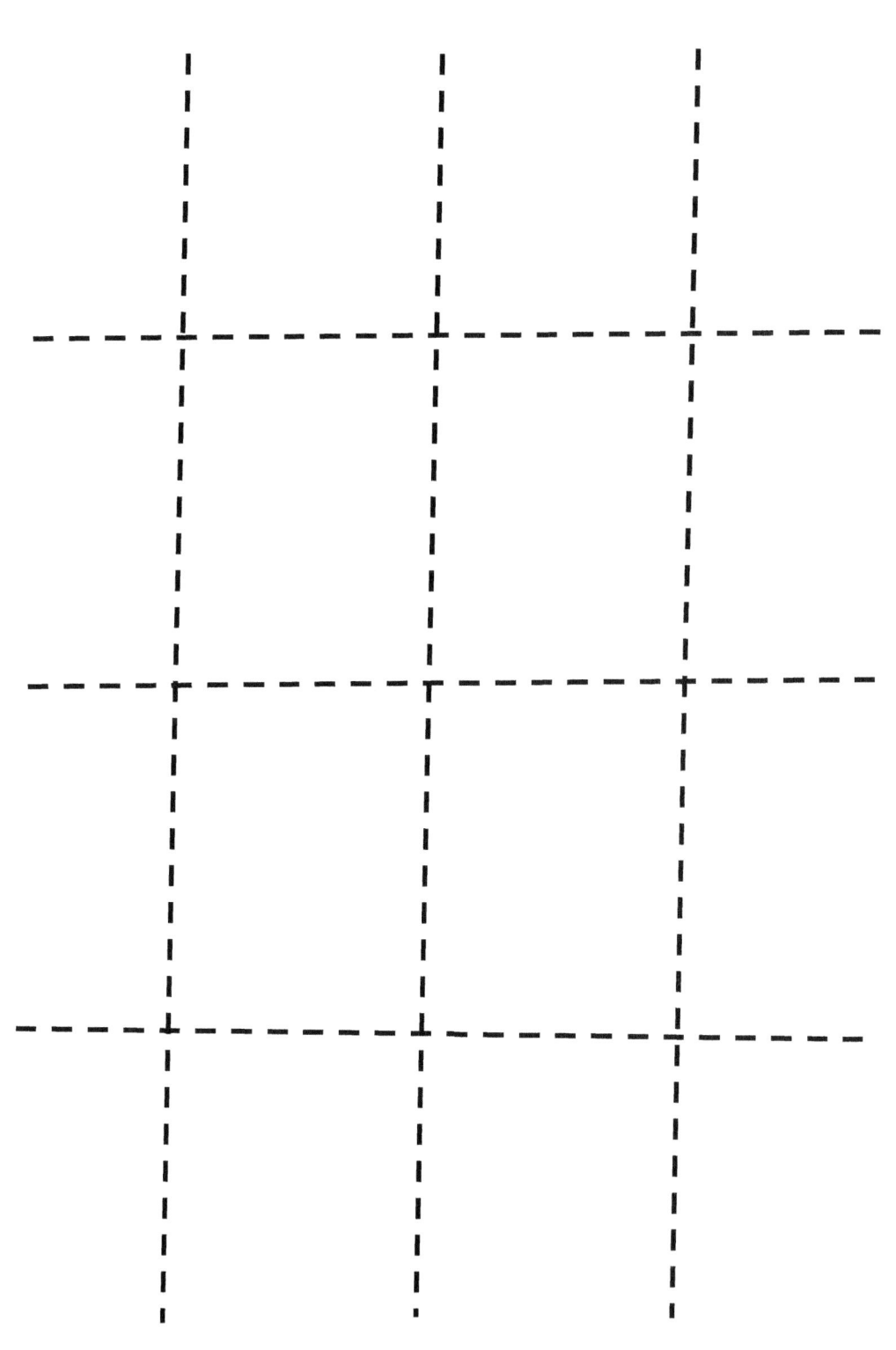

DRAW LINES
ON THE BUS, A TRAIN

WHILE IN MOTION.
WHILE WALKING.

Make this page POP UP

SCRIBBLE WILDLY, VIOLENTLY,
WITH RECKLESS ABANDON

Write carelessly. Now.

Wrap something with this page.

Like this

DOCUMENT YOUR DINNER
(RUB, SMEAR, SPLATTER YOUR FOOD)
- -
USE THIS PAGE AS A NAPKIN

Create A Drawing Using A Piece (Or Several Pieces) Of Your Hair

TIE A STRING TO THE SPINE OF THIS BOOK.

Swing Wildly

LET IT HIT THE WALLS.

ASK A FRIEND TO DO SOMETHING DESTRUCTIVE TO THIS PAGE. DON'T LOOK

MAKE A PAPER AiRPLANE

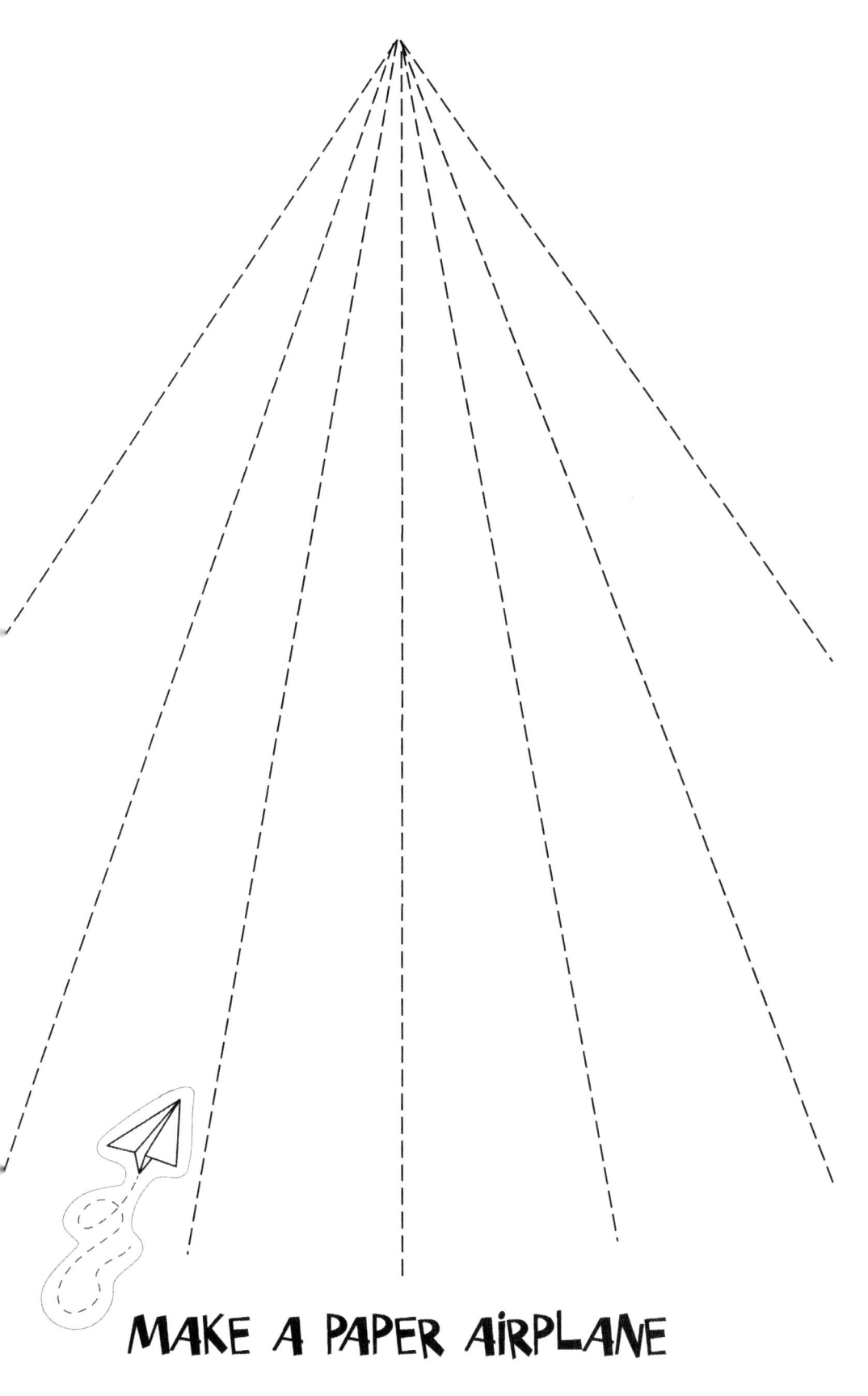

END OF THE JOURNAL

THANK YOU
for spending time together

Printed in Great Britain
by Amazon